Donated in memory of
Wilton Hunter Talley &
Elizabeth Almond Talley
By Julia Talley Draucker
January, 1993

Celebrating Independence Day

By: Shelly Nielsen
Illustrated by: Marie-Claude Monchaux

Published by Abdo & Daughters, 6535 Cecilia Circle, Edina, Minnesota 55439.

Library bound edition distributed by Rockbottom Books, Pentagon Tower, P.O. Box 36036, Minneapolis, Minnesota 55435.

Copyright © 1992 by Abdo Consulting Group, Inc., Pentagon Tower, P.O. Box 36036, Minneapolis, Minnesota 55435. International copyrights reserved in all countries. No part of this book may be reproduced in any form without written permission from the publisher. Printed in the United States.

Edited by: Rosemary Wallner

LIBRARY OF CONGRESS CATALOGING-IN-PUBLICATION DATA

Nielsen, Shelly, 1958-
  Independence Day / written by Shelly Nielsen; [edited by Rosemary Wallner]
  p. cm. -- (Holiday celebrations)
  Summary: Rhyming text introduces aspects of this important national holiday.
  ISBN 1-56239-071-6
  1. Fourth of July celebrations--Juvenile literature. [1. Fourth of July.] I. Wallner, Rosemary, 1964-
II. Title. III. Series: Nielsen, Shelly, 1958- Holiday celebrations.
E286.A145   1992   394.2"68473--dc20   91-73030

International Standard Book Number:
1-56239-071-6

Library of Congress Catalog Card Number:
91-73030

Celebrating Independence Day

It's Hot!

Whew, it's <u>hot</u> . . .
and it's only ten o'clock.
Fourth of July
must be on its way
when bare toes sizzle on sidewalks.
So here's what I do —
put on a bathing suit,
turn on the sprinkler —
scream, run through,
I hop and skip and take a jump . . .
Oooo!
Goosebumps.

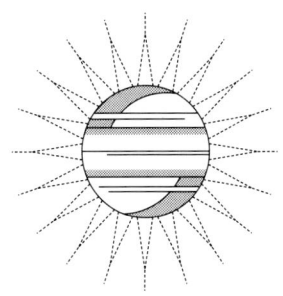

Why?

Grandpa —
Why do we celebrate Independence Day?

So we can yell and cheer and watch parades,
swish cool fans in the oak tree's shade,
chug-a-lug cold lemonade.
But mostly why we celebrate
is to remember the beginning of the United States.

Luscious Lemonade

I love luscious lemonade.
Do you love it, too?
Then let's make a glass
from lemons cut in two.
Squeeze and squeeze
out all the juice,
then stir in sugar and taste.
Ooops . . .
I can tell we need more sugar.
You made a sour face!

Flags for the Fourth

I helped Mr. Himmelman
hang out an American flag.
We carefully uncurled it
and at first it just sagged;
but then the wind lifted it up
and made it flap and wave.
    Stars and stripes,
      red, blue, and white.
I waved back.

Sam Hates Firecrackers

My dog Sam
(part beagle, part mutt)
is under my bed
and won't come out.
Just wait till you hear
what makes him quiver and quake —
firecrackers make him shiver and shake.
Hey, Sam, you scardy-dog:
want to borrow some ear plugs?

Pack-A-Picnic

We're packing a picnic —
what will we take?
    Pickles,
    chips,
    and chocolate cake.
Corn-on-the-cob.
A salad of eggs and potatoes.
    Burgers,
    buns,
    and tomatoes.
Now all that we need for our barbecue
is someone to eat it —
me and you!

Volleyball!

One . . . two . . . three . . . *serve!*
When the volleyball flies —
I put up my hands,
close my eyes,
and . . .
push!
        THUNK!
                WHOOSH!
There it goes!
I stand on tiptoe
and watch Bonnie
send it flying back.
Again I jump . . .
and give that ball a whack!
It sails over the net
and lands — SMACK!
Hey! It's a score!
Just listen to that crowd roar!

We huff and puff,
slap hands, and shout,
(except Bonnie, who pouts).

Now give the ball to Ben.
We're ready to serve, again.

Who Wants Watermelon?

Take a bite
of a watermelon slice.
Mmmmm . . .
It's cold as ice!
Watermelon is so sweet
it makes you laugh just to eat it.
So while you wear a sticky grin
and melon juice drips off your chin —
hold a seed between your lips,
carefully take aim . . . and spit!

More Mosquito Bites

Bzzz!
Slap!
Scratch-scratch-scratch!
Another mosquito bite — *oh, drat.*
If that mean mosquito would just hold still,
I'd sprinkle on itching powder
so she'd know how it feels.

Ice Cream Magic

We put cream and sugar and other good stuff
in an ice cream maker
packed with salt and ice.
We all took turns spinning the crank —
first Daddy, then Gramps, then Uncle Frank.
I cranked till my muscles were sore
then I cranked,
and cranked,
and cranked some more.
Finally . . .
Daddy announced, "It's all done!"
Mama brought spoons and bowls for everyone.
A giant scoop for me, please.
I love ice cream!

Sparkler Dance

When Mama lights it
my sparkler spits sparks,
and dazzles my eyes
in the dark.
I holler and whoop,
write my name
do loopty-loops,
twist and shout
until
at last
my
sparkler sputters . . .
and goes out.

Fireflies and Crickets

The fireflies and crickets
are having their own Independence Day;
The fireflies blink their silver fireworks lights
while the crickets chirp away.

Fantastic Fireworks

Lay back —
feel the grass,
cool and prickly,
tickle your neck.
Ready, set, there they go!
BOOM! CRACK! It's a fireworks show!
Oooh! Ahhhh!
A flower of red!
Then gems of gold
showering our heads!
Diamond lights
to catch in our hands . . .
but they disappear
before they land.

Home Again

We all drive home
from the park.
Mommy steers
through the dark.
My sunburn hurts,
my bug bites itch;
I'm tired out,
and tired in;
I'm sticky and hot,
and burning red . . .
Wasn't it fun?
Let's do it again!

LOCUST GROVE ELEM. LIBRARY

9750